THE LITTLE
HERB
TIPS

WILLIAM FORTT

THE LITTLE BOOK OF
HERB
TIPS

WILLIAM FORTT

Absolute Press

First published in Great Britain in 2006 by
Absolute Press
Scarborough House, 29 James Street West
Bath BA1 2BT, England
Phone 44 (0) 1225 316013 **Fax** 44 (0) 1225 445836
E-mail info@absolutepress.co.uk
Web www.absolutepress.co.uk

Reprinted 2008.

A catalogue record of this book is available
from the British Library

ISBN 13: 9781904573364

Printed and bound in China by 1010.

How can a man die who has sage
in his garden?

Arab proverb

When you've got the choice, use

fresh herbs

in cooking rather than dried. They

give a longer and more vivid flavour

to the dish – and a much better colour.

2

Keep dried herbs in dark glass containers

with tight fitting lids. This will help to preserve the precious aromas, protected from light and moisture in the air.

3

The very best place to

store your
dried herbs is
in the freezer,
where their flavour will last longer.
Remember to take out the container in plenty
of time, so that it can warm to room temperature.
This stops moisture from the warm air of the
kitchen from condensing on the leaves.

4

Fresh herbs from hot countries,

such as basil,

hate the cold.

Shock from the chill of a refrigerator may ruin them, so keep them at room temperature – preferably with their stems in water.

5

Some herbs are more suited to drying than others.

Those from dry Mediterranean areas, such as thyme, rosemary, oregano and bay leaf, keep much of their flavour in the drying process. Moister herbs, such as basil, tarragon and parsley, lose most of theirs.

6

In general, **add small-leaved fresh herbs** to the dish **near the end of the cooking time.**

Prolonged heat tends to destroy many of the natural vitamins they contain. Herbs with bigger leaves can be cooked for longer.

The most important part of a herb

is its aroma. Smell is a vital element in what we recognize as the 'flavour' of a dish. A herb's aromas are contained in chemicals which easily evaporate into the air (which is why we can smell them). So store them well away from heat or pressure, which will speed up this evaporation.

8

Freezing is an effective way of

preserving fresh herbs

– as long as you don't mind what they look like. The freezing creates ice crystals which damage the vegetable tissue, often making the herbs squashy and dark when they are defrosted.

Most fresh herbs can be stored for a day or two in the fridge.

Put them in plastic bags but leave the ends open. This will prevent mould spores growing on the damp leaves.

10

If you've got a garden,

grow your own perennial herbs, which will give a

supply year after year with minimal attention.
Mint grows anywhere (though confine it in a pot).
Sage, thyme, marjoram and rosemary are also
pretty tough, and can make attractive bushes.

11

It's easy to

dry your own garden herbs.

The best season to harvest them is early summer, when the flavour is strongest. And the best time of day for cutting is mid-morning, after the dew has gone but before the sun is too hot.

12

Tie small-leaved herbs, such as thyme and marjoram, **in loose bundles.** Hang them up to dry in a shady, warmish place indoors (not too warm, or the aroma will disappear with the water). Wrap each bundle in muslin to keep off dust and insects.

13

Herbs such as **coriander, dill and fennel can be harvested for their seeds** in late summer. Cut off the ripe seed-heads with a good length of stalk and hang up to dry. Then shake out the seeds onto a clean dry surface. Spread them out and leave to dry for another couple of hours before storing in a container.

Herbs with large leaves,

such as sage and mint,

need very careful drying.

Separate the leaves and spread them on a wire rack covered in muslin. Place in a dark, dry room for two or three weeks, gently turning them once or twice.

15

Once your herbs are well dried, they need to be crushed.

Spread them out on a flat dry surface and run a rolling pin over them. Pick out the stalks and any other unwanted bits before you store them.

16

Always
remember to label each of your herb jars.

A lot of dried herbs can look the same to an inexperienced eye, and some smell remarkably similar. Correct labelling now will avoid confusion in six months' time.

Home-dried herbs should keep their flavour for up to one year. But commercially

dried herbs

from a shop will probably be a few months old by the time you buy them.

Replace your supply every six months – at least.

18

Feeling fragile, low or hung over? This simple **herb soup** from the south of France is known to locals as 'life-saving boiled water' and **is a superb tonic.** Peel and crush a whole head of garlic, then boil for 15 minutes with 1 litre (2 pints) of water, a handful of sage leaves, a bay leaf and a little olive oil and salt. Serve with toasted bread.

19

Chop fresh herbs by hand with a sharp knife

or a mezzaluna. Try to do this carefully and neatly. Wild chopping with a blunt edge will simply crush the herb's fibres and cause blackening. Whizzing in a food processor is even worse. This will mix in too much oxygen, and spoil the vivid aroma of the leaves.

20

A ready supply of fresh parsley is a joy for any cook. It's an annual plant, so you can

grow your own parsley in pots or beds, indoors

or out. Only buy seeds of flat-leaved parsley (forget the curly kind) and soak them in cold water overnight to speed up germination. Sow a new batch every month, and you'll never run out.

21

A few leaves of basil transform many a salad. It is not too difficult to grow, although a very fussy plant. Sow seeds well spaced out in a pot on a sunny windowsill.

Basil hates being fiddled with,

so do not transplant the seedlings. If the plants get infested with aphids, put the pots outside for a few hours.

22

Make your own basil pesto

– it will be much better than anything in a jar. Put about 100g (3$\frac{1}{2}$oz) of fresh basil leaves in a food processor with 120ml (4fl oz) olive oil, 25g (1oz) of pine nuts, three peeled cloves of garlic and a good pinch of salt. Blend briefly, then add about 50g (2oz) of grated Parmesan cheese and whizz again.

23

Chervil is a strangely neglected herb.
Both its leaves and flavour are very elegant
and delicate, giving off a subtle hint of aniseed.
But beware – it loses pungency very quickly
with cooking. Chervil adds

a heavenly touch to uncomplicated dishes such as scrambled eggs and omelettes.

24

Bay trees are not just ornaments in hotel lobbies. A small bush will survive the winter outside if protected from the fiercest frosts, and will give you a year-round supply of fresh bay leaves –

a delight for any cook.

The leaves have a hundred uses, from flavouring meat stocks to burning on a barbecue.

25

Poor Man's Potatoes is a Spanish dish which makes

simple use of the potency of bay.

Sauté a sliced onion slowly in oil, adding a chopped green pepper and then three or four bay leaves. Put in roughly chopped potatoes (and chunks of ham or chorizo if available), cover and cook for 20 minutes.

26

Fresh herbs in a stuffing can transform a humdrum roast turkey.

Sauté two chopped onions in plenty of butter and oil, then put in a bowl and mix with 450g (1lb) of breadcrumbs and lashings of chopped parsley, thyme, winter savory, marjoram, sage and lemon balm.
When it's cold, stuff your bird.

27

When buying garlic, check the quality carefully.

By late winter, you will find a lot of bulbs drying up or going mouldy. **Give the heads a good squeeze.**

If you feel anything soft or hollow, or see any black patches, don't buy them. Good quality garlic should be hard and even in colour.

28

Peeling garlic can be a fiddly job.

Speed things up by first crushing the clove under the flat of the knife blade, pressing with the heel of your hand (carefully). You will hear a crunch as the garlic splits. Now slice off each end and the outer skin should come away easily.

29

Crush

peeled garlic cloves

with a pestle and mortar.

This will create the sweetest flavour.
Avoid those two-handled garlic presses,
which simply mangle the garlic and produce
a much harsher result.

A bouquet garni is one of the classic combinations of herbs in French cooking. Tie together a little bundle containing a bay leaf plus sprigs of thyme and parsley. This **can be used to flavour soups and stews** – and is easy to remove before serving.

31

Fines herbes

is a mixture of finely chopped chervil, parsley, tarragon and chives which

can be added to all kinds of delicate dishes.

Omelettes, grilled white fish and chicken can be transformed by its light touch.

32

Herbes de Provence is a classic French combination. The mixture usually contains chopped rosemary, coriander, fennel, basil, thyme, marjoram and lavender (a surprising, potent and much neglected herb). They are

an essential flavouring for game or duck confit,

but try adding them to bread dough as well.

33

The speediest of all pasta sauces

calls for just two ingredients – fresh sage leaves and butter. Melt 110g (4oz) of unsalted butter over a gentle heat. When it froths, add a good handful or two of chopped sage and cook for two minutes. This sage butter is especially good for coating ravioli or tortellini.

34

Spaghetti with fresh herbs is a simple classic.

While the pasta is boiling, fry sliced garlic in olive oil for one minute. Then bung in two handfuls of whatever herbs you fancy (choose three or four from parsley, marjoram, rosemary, oregano, rocket or basil). Cook for another minute. Drain the pasta (leaving enough water to moisten it) and stir into the sauce.

35

Hyssop is a sadly forgotten herb in most kitchens. But its unusual minty, mothbally smell and subtly bitter taste are worth discovering. It **adds a stunning new dimension to salads,** and enhances the taste of rabbit stews and (amazingly enough) fruit pies.

36

Mint

in its many varieties

is easy to grow,

and has far more interesting uses than vinegary
old mint sauce. It is an essential ingredient in
the bulgur wheat salad tabbouleh, as well
as chilled yoghurt and cucumber soup.
Some vegetables go perfectly with mint,
notably potatoes, fresh peas, courgettes
and – best of all – aubergines.

37

The people of Crete eat a lot of

purslane

– and their diet is said to be the healthiest in the world. As well as having

a deliciously citric taste, the fleshy

leaves of purslane are a rich source of iron and omega-3 fatty acids. Eat them raw in salads, together with cucumber, parsley and tomatoes, with a yoghurt dressing.

38

Basil wine is a traditional tonic from the south of France. **Soothing for the stomach,** it also tastes amazingly good. Pour a bottle of light red wine into a litre jar, and add a handful of basil leaves and a chunk of orange peel. Make 150ml (5fl oz) of sugar and water syrup and pour that in. Cork the bottle and leave for at least three weeks.

39

Herbal teas are highly valued all over the world

for their soothing and medicinal properties. Simply put your chosen herb (rosemary, lime flowers, camomile, sage or lavender seeds are among the best) into a warmed teapot. Pour on hot water and leave to infuse.

40

Rosemary goes remarkably well with partridge.

Put a good sprig inside each bird, then wrap them in bacon and brown in oil, surrounded with onions and more rosemary. Chuck in a glass of red wine and simmer for 15 minutes. Serve the birds with the strained and reduced sauce.

41

The volatile oils of herbs can be gently extracted

by steeping them in vinegar. Tarragon, dill, thyme and rosemary are among the best for flavouring vinegar. Gently crush a handful of the herbs first, then place them in a jar (easier to fill than a bottle). Fill up with a good white wine vinegar, stopper tightly and leave for one month.

42

Home-made horseradish sauce tastes far better

than the commercial stuff. Peel and grate the horseradish root, then whizz in the food processor with lemon juice and cream. A little sugar broadens the flavour.

43

Dill is the quintessential herb for fish

– most famously for gravlax, the Swedish version of pickled raw salmon. Mix 4 tablespoons of chopped dill with 2 tablespoons each of sea salt and sugar, plus a generous grinding of black pepper. Line a dish with clingfilm, lay salmon fillets on it, pour over the mixture and wrap the clingfilm round the fish. Refrigerate for at least 12 hours.

44

The perfect tomato salsa

can only be made with fresh coriander leaves. Assemble your own from chopped onion, ripe tomatoes (skinned, deseeded and chopped), chopped mint, a couple of chopped green chillies, fresh lime juice, a pinch of sugar and a whole bunch of coriander. Blend in the processor if you like, but some like it coarse.

45

Always eat chives in their raw state

– never cooked, because they lose all their potency. Snip them up with scissors onto salads or soups. Even better, mix with sour cream or Greek yoghurt to adorn baked potatoes.

46

Keep an **aloe vera** plant in a pot on your kitchen windowsill. You can't actually eat it, but it's

wonderful for simple first aid.

If you scald or burn yourself, cut off the tip of a fleshy leaf and rub the cut end on the wound. You'll find it wonderfully soothing.

47

If you are marinating fish

before grilling,

suit the herb to the variety

when you make the marinade. Fish with white flesh and delicate flavour, such as bass and bream, go best with feathery fennel leaves. Stronger-tasting fish, such as sardine or mackerel, need a punchier herb like oregano.

48

The best part of a **borage** plant is its splendid blue flowers. They add a hint of cucumbery glamour to salads and soups. You can also freeze them inside ice cubes ready to **pop into a jug of Pimms.**

49

Sorrel is a wonderfully bracing herb, with the tart flavour of spinach but more delicacy. It **goes perfectly with eggs.**

Finely shred 300g (10$\frac{1}{2}$oz) of young sorrel leaves and cook gently in butter until you have a smooth sauce. Stir in some double cream, season and pour over 6 hard-boiled eggs. Bake for about 15 minutes.

50

Watercress makes one of the best of all soups.

Peel and chop 150g (5½oz) of potatoes and an onion and boil in 600ml (1 pint) of water or chicken stock and an equal amount of creamy milk. When the vegetables are soft, add 225g (8oz) of chopped watercress leaves. Cook for 5 more minutes, purée and season.

William Fortt

William Fortt is a gardener of long standing, whose cottage garden in Wiltshire, is famed for the beauty of its rare plants and the wonders of its many varieties of culinary and medicinal herbs. He has been an author for more than 30 years, with many books to his name.

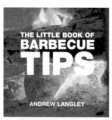

THE LITTLE BOOK OF
BARBECUE
TIPS

ANDREW LANGLEY

THE LITTLE BOOK OF
BEER
TIPS

ANDREW LANGLEY

THE LITTLE BOOK OF
HERB
TIPS

WILLIAM FORTT

THE LITTLE BOOK OF
POKER
TIPS

PETER FRENCH

THE LITTLE BOOK OF
GARDENING
TIPS

WILLIAM FORTT

THE LITTLE BOOK OF
CHEFS'
TIPS

RICHARD MAGGS

THE LITTLE BOOK OF
SPICE
TIPS

ANDREW LANGLEY

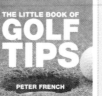

THE LITTLE BOOK OF
GOLF
TIPS

PETER FRENCH

THE LITTLE BOOK OF
TIPS
SERIES

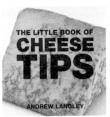

THE LITTLE BOOK OF
CHEESE TIPS

ANDREW LANGLEY

THE LITTLE BOOK OF
WINE TIPS

ANDREW LANGLEY

THE LITTLE BOOK OF
AGA TIPS²

RICHARD MAGGS

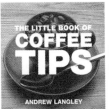

THE LITTLE BOOK OF
COFFEE TIPS

ANDREW LANGLEY

THE LITTLE BOOK OF
TEA TIPS

ANDREW LANGLEY

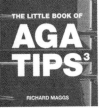

THE LITTLE BOOK OF
AGA TIPS³

RICHARD MAGGS

THE LITTLE BOOK OF
AGA TIPS

RICHARD MAGGS

THE LITTLE BOOK OF
CHRISTMAS AGA TIPS

RICHARD MAGGS

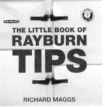

THE LITTLE BOOK OF
RAYBURN TIPS

RICHARD MAGGS

THE LITTLE BOOK OF
BRIDGE TIPS
CHRIS JONES

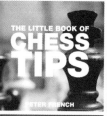
THE LITTLE BOOK OF
CHESS TIPS
PETER FRENCH

THE LITTLE BOOK OF
FISHING TIPS
MICK DEVENISH

THE LITTLE BOOK OF
GREEN TIPS
WILLIAM FORTT

THE LITTLE BOOK OF
KITTEN TIPS
ANDREW LANGLEY

PAUL HARTLEY
THE LITTLE BOOK OF
MARMITE TIPS

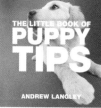
THE LITTLE BOOK OF
PUPPY TIPS
ANDREW LANGLEY

THE LITTLE BOOK OF
WHISKY TIPS
ANDREW LANGLEY

THE LITTLE BOOK OF
TRAVEL TIPS
MEGAN DEVENISH

Little Books of Tips from Absolute Press

Aga Tips
Aga Tips 2
Aga Tips 3
Backgammon Tips
Barbecue Tips
Beer Tips
Bread Tips
Bridge Tips
Cake Decorating Tips
Cheese Tips
Chefs' Tips
Chess Tips
Christmas Aga Tips
Coffee Tips
Fishing Tips
Gardening Tips
Golf Tips
Green Tips

Hair Tips
Herb Tips
Houseplant Tips
Kitten Tips
Marmite Tips
Nail Tips
Olive Oil Tips
Poker Tips
Puppy Tips
Rayburn Tips
Scrabble Tips
Spice Tips
Tea Tips
Travel Tips
Vinegar Tips
Whisky Tips
Wine Tips

**All titles: £2.99 /
112 pages**